LITTLE QUICK FIX:

STATISTICAL SIGNIFICANCE

#LittleQuickFix

Sara Miller McCune founded SAGE Publishing in 1965 to support the dissemination of usable knowledge and educate a global community. SAGE publishes more than 1000 journals and over 800 new books each year, spanning a wide range of subject areas. Our growing selection of library products includes archives, data, case studies and video. SAGE remains majority owned by our founder and after her lifetime will become owned by a charitable trust that secures the company's continued independence.

Los Angeles | London | New Delhi | Singapore | Washington DC | Melbourne

LITTLE QUICK FIX: STATISTICAL SIGNIFICANCE

John
MacInnes

Los Angeles | London | New Delhi
Singapore | Washington DC | Melbourne

Los Angeles | London | New Delhi
Singapore | Washington DC | Melbourne

SAGE Publications Ltd
1 Oliver's Yard
55 City Road
London EC1Y 1SP

SAGE Publications Inc.
2455 Teller Road
Thousand Oaks, California 91320

SAGE Publications India Pvt Ltd
B 1/I 1 Mohan Cooperative Industrial Area
Mathura Road
New Delhi 110 044

SAGE Publications Asia-Pacific Pte Ltd
3 Church Street
#10-04 Samsung Hub
Singapore 049483

© John MacInnes 2019

First published 2019

Editor: Aly Owen
Production editor: Ian Antcliff
Marketing manager: Ben Griffin-Sherwood
Design: Shaun Mercier
Typeset by: C&M Digitals (P) Ltd, Chennai, India
Printed in the UK

Library of Congress Control Number: 2018961584

British Library Cataloguing in Publication data

A catalogue record for this book is available
from the British Library

ISBN 978-1-5264-6678-5

Contents

Everything in this book 4

Section 1   What is statistical significance? 9

Section 2   Why do samples have to be random? 21

Section 3   What is a normal distribution? 35

Section 4   What is a standard error? 59

Section 5   How do I calculate confidence
             intervals with standard errors? 73

Section 6   What is a *p*-value? 89

Section 7   What does a significant p-value
             actually mean? 103

Glossary 118

Everything in this book!

Section 1 Because populations are so big, we infer population characteristics from samples. Information from samples is not perfect, so we describe potentially interesting results as statistically significant.

Section 2 In a random sample every member of a population has a known chance of being included. Only random samples allow us to estimate the values of population parameters.

Section 3 In a normal distribution, most of the observations are close to the mean, and as we move away from it, there are fewer and fewer of them. A neat formula tells us the proportion of cases near the mean.

Section 4 Sampling distributions make all the estimates we have from random samples possible. From them we can calculate standard errors, which tell us how close to the population parameter a sample estimate is likely to be.

Section 5 Using standard errors, we can identify a range of estimates that we can be confident includes the population parameter we wish to know.

Section 6 When we test a null hypothesis, we get a p-value. If this value is low enough, we reject the null hypothesis and have a statIstically significant finding.

Section 7 We can never be 100% sure that any individual result from a sample gives us the right information about a population. The p-values, confidence and significance describe how good our procedures for getting that information have been.

Section

1

Infer population characteristics from samples

What is statistical significance?

A

10 SEC summary

Statistical significance tells us what we can infer about a target population from what we find in a sample.

summary

Inference and significance

Modern societies are large, complex and change continuously and rapidly. This makes describing or measuring them rather difficult.

Instead we identify target populations, draw random samples from them, and then infer from these samples what the target population must be like.

We call findings *statistically significant* if we think our sample results tell us something about the population.

People sometimes find statistical significance difficult. Partly this is because the language is old fashioned, and partly because the logic is counter-intuitive. However, this Little Quick Fix takes you through it in straightforward steps.

YOU CAN'T MEASURE EVERYONE AND EVERYTHING

Societies and their economies change constantly. Monitoring and measuring such change directly would be impossible. Collecting even the simplest information about tens of millions of people, or billions of economic transactions, would be a hopeless task.

Yet we need fast and accurate data on myriads of topics to keep societies functioning.

Many measurements we might want to make – about whether a new drug has side effects, or whether an anti-poverty policy works – are expensive and cumbersome. We could not test every potential patient every time a new drug was invented!

The answer to this problem is to identify target populations and sample them.

Target populations can be objects, activities, events, experimental results or anything else, as well as people. We call the population characteristics that interest us *parameters*.

Because populations are too big to measure, we cannot describe their parameters directly. They are unknown.

We use our sample to estimate these parameters. This is inference.

HOW TO KNOW YOUR ESTIMATE IS ANY GOOD

However, we also need to know how good this estimate is likely to be.

One way of doing this is to decide whether a result is *statistically significant*.

The power of statistical significance

We call a positive result or finding *statistically significant* if we think there is a *low* probability of getting it in our sample when the result was in fact negative in the target population.

Getting a positive result by demonstrating a *low* probability of *not* having a negative result appears to be a confusing double negative. Such logic is the best that inference can do. But as we'll see, it is actually very powerful.

STATISTICAL SIGNIFICANCE DOES NOT EQUAL IMPORTANCE

However, statistically significant does not necessarily mean important.

The meaning of words in English is constantly evolving. When statisticians first used the term 'significant' it simply meant 'signals'. That is the meaning it still has in statistics. Elsewhere the meaning of significant has morphed into 'important'. This misleads people into thinking that a 'statistically significant' result must be an important one.

Not so!

Statistical *signi*ficance *sign*als that a finding is worth investigating further.

To understand the logic of inference, we look first at *random samples*.

Fill in the blanks with the correct term. Look back through this section or check the glossary if you need more help.

A group of objects or people we want to measure is a ....
population

A selection from a target population is called a ....

Samples are used to estimate unknown ....

A significant result in a .... is a signal that there is a
.... probability that we'd not also get that result in the
.... if we could measure it.

.... is the process of using samples to measure
population parameters

Significant means ....

Estimate the values of population parameters

Section

2

Why do I have to use a random sample?

summary

We need random samples to estimate population
parameters, because only random samples allow
us to produce a sampling distribution.

Random means a known probability of selection

For inference to work, we need a way to work out how good any sample is from the characteristics of the sample itself. (We cannot use the population, because we cannot measure it!)

We can do this if a sample is random.

A random sample is one in which every member of the target population has the same probability of being drawn.

Samples are rarely purely random in practice, because we hardly ever have a complete and accurate list of any target population. However, samples that come close to this work well enough.

USING SAMPLES TO MEASURE POPULATION VARIATION

Any newspaper or news bulletin contains information like

- There were 450,000 cases of flu in Japan last winter

- 1.5 million luxury cars were sold in the USA last year

- This summer is set to be the warmest in Europe for 40 years

Nobody tracked down everyone in Japan to ask if they had the flu, or counted every car sold. Temperature varies locally, by the time of day and from one day to the next – measuring it completely would be impossible.

Instead we take a *target population* we want to measure (people in Japan last winter, cars sold in the USA last year, temperatures in Europe) and draw a *sample* from it.

HOW TO KNOW IF A SAMPLE IS REPRESENTATIVE OF ITS TARGET POPULATION

Maybe we just happen to pick people who'd had the flu or places that enjoyed good summer weather.

We cannot check the representativeness of our sample by comparing it with the population, because, as we saw in the previous section, it is too big to measure.

The ingenious answer to this puzzle comes from randomness.

We draw our sample in such a way that *every member of the target population has the same probability of being selected*. A random sample is like a fair lottery, with the prizes being selection into the sample.

WHY BOTHER WITH RANDOM SAMPLES?

Ensuring that a sample is random is not easy. Why go to all the bother?

If a sample is random we can calculate what range of estimates *every possible* sample of the same size would produce for some population parameters. This is called a *sampling distribution*.

We explain what these are in the next section!

In practice the probabilities of population members being sampled need not be *equal*, as long they are *known*. Sometimes we include extra examples of rare members of a population, to ensure that we have enough for our analysis.

A perfectly random sample is often impossible to achieve in practice, but *approximately* random samples work well enough.

METHODS FOR FINDING A RANDOM SAMPLE

Random samples are usually produced in one of two ways.

1. Listing and numbering the entire target population, and then randomly generating numbers to select members for the sample

2. When listing is not feasible, 'capturing' population members in any way that gives them an equal chance of being 'caught'

FINDING RANDOM SAMPLES

You want to draw a random sample of the students at a university. Which of the following methods would produce an approximately random sample?

1 You put up an advert in the student union asking for volunteers

2 You take every student whose surname starts with M

3 You go to the refectory at lunchtime and select everyone there

4 You select every student coming out of the lectures held at 11 a.m.

5 You obtain a list of all the students, randomly pick a place to start near the beginning of the list, and select every 100th student in the list after that

6 You pick the class representatives across all the modules offered at the university

7 You move randomly about the campus, picking every 10th student you meet

ANSWERS

Only method 5 would be random.

Surnames vary by culture. You might get many Scottish students (all those Mc's and Mac's) but few Chinese students.

Certain kinds of students will be more likely to (1) volunteer, (3) take lunch in the refectory, (4) attend 11 o'clock lectures, (6) be class reps or (7) be anywhere on campus.

Section

In a normal distribution most observations are close to the mean

What is
a normal
distribution?

A

10 SEC summary

In a *normal distribution* of data, most observations are close to the average, and their number decreases as we move away from it.

Normal distributions have most observations near the mean

Any normal distribution is described by just two numbers: its *mean* (average) and *standard deviation*.

The standard deviation measures the *spread* of any data: that is, whether observations cluster closely towards the mean for all observations or are widely dispersed above and below it.

In a normal distribution, 95% of observations lie within two standard deviations of the mean.

DEFINING A NORMAL DISTRIBUTION

Normal distributions describe a collection of measurements, observations, data points or results where most are found near the average and the number decreases as we move away from it.

HOW TO READ A
NORMAL DISTRIBUTION

Figure 1 shows the height measurements to the nearest half-inch of 20,000 soldiers, made during the American Civil War.

The heights are shown along the *horizontal* axis. The *vertical* length of each bar represents the number of soldiers of each height. For example, the bar coloured blue shows that about 1450 soldiers were 5 feet 6 inches; the bar coloured red shows that about 30 soldiers were 6 feet 1½ inches tall; and so on.

The longest bars are found in the middle, coinciding with the mean height of the soldiers: 5 feet 7 inches. Most soldiers are close to average height.

As we move above or below this average the number of soldiers decreases.

At the extremes of the distribution there are very few soldiers indeed. The tallest solider was actually 6 feet 7 inches and the shortest 4 feet tall.

The soldiers' heights are an example of a normal distribution.

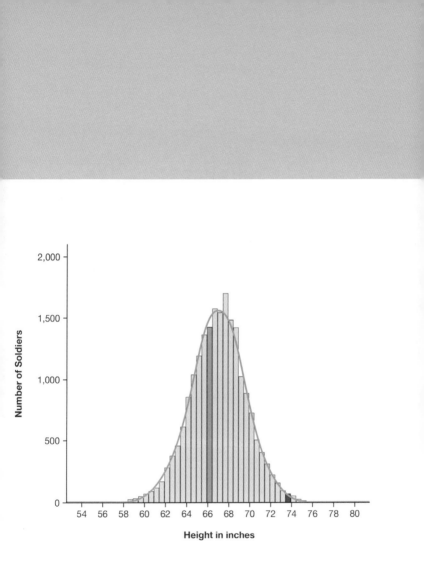

Figure 1 **Heights of union soldiers in inches**

NORMAL DISTRIBUTIONS AND STANDARD DEVIATIONS

Normal distributions can be defined by just two numbers: the mean (the arithmetic average) and the standard deviation (a measure of the spread of values).

Small standard deviations produce a steeper 'hump' as measurements cluster closely around the mean. Large standard deviations produce flatter humps.

For soldiers' heights the standard deviation is small at only 2.6 inches.

CALCULATING THE SPREAD OF YOUR DATA

Because all normal distributions have a similar shape, a formula describes where we find almost all the observations.

About 95% of observations are within two standard deviations above or below the average.

Therefore about 95% of these soldiers will have heights between

5 feet 7 inches - (2 × 2.5) inches = 5 feet 2 inches
5 feet 7 inches + (2 × 2.5) inches = 6 feet 0 inches

So

- most soldiers are near average height
- 95% of soldiers are between 5 feet 2 inches and 6 feet
- only 5% of soldiers are shorter or taller than this range
- virtually no soldiers are very much shorter or taller than this

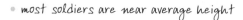

HOW STANDARD DEVIATION RELATES TO RANDOMNESS

This can be put another way. If I pick a single soldier *at random*

- the most likely result is a soldier near average height

- there is a 95% chance of getting one between 5 feet 2 inches and 6 feet tall

- there is a 5% chance of getting a shorter or taller soldier

- there is virtually no chance of getting an extremely short or tall soldier

Note that all these statements are summary descriptions of *all* the soldiers. *After* I have picked a soldier, there is nothing probable about their height. Either they are between 5 feet 2 inches and 6 feet or they are not.

This might seem like splitting hairs, but as we will see later, this distinction is important.

USING THE 95% RULE

You can use the 95% rule to work out where any observation in a distribution can be found

- Take the mean of the distribution

- *Add* twice the standard deviation *to* the mean

- Subtract twice the standard deviation *from* the mean

    Any observation *between* these two numbers is in the middle 95%

    Any observation *above* the first number is in the top 2.5%

    Any observation *below* the second number is in the bottom 2.5%

HOW TO USE
THE 95% RULE

I get 64 for my end-of-term exam so I'm chuffed…until I hear that a lot of people got high marks. I'm told that the marks were normally distributed, and the average mark was 77 with a standard deviation of marks. Two hundred students taking the exam. How well did I do? Use the normal distribution to find out.

What is the mean of the distribution?

___

(77)

Add twice the standard deviation to the mean

___ + ___ = ___

(77 + 12 = 89)

Subtract twice the standard deviation from the mean

___ – ___ = ___

(59 = ZI – tt)

This means 95% of students will have marks between ___ and ___.

(68 pนɒ S9)

So my mark of 64 means that I am in

(a) The top 2.5% of the class ☐

(b) The middle 95% of the class ☐

(c) The bottom 2.5% of the class ☐

(ɔ)

Well, assessment marks may be a poor measure of real ability or understanding, and what I got in this exam may not predict how well I do in the *next* one.

In my next exam I only get 57. Once again I'm told that the marks were normally distributed, but this time the average was 50 and the standard deviation was 4. Should I be pleased? Work it out!

What is the mean of the distribution?

___

(50)

Add twice the standard deviation to the mean

___ + ___ = ___

(58 = 8 + 50)

Subtract twice the standard deviation from the mean

___ - ___ = ___

(42 = 8 - 50)

This means 95% of students will have marks between ___ and ___.

(42 and 58)

So my mark of 57 means I am in

(a) The top 2.5% of the class ☐

(b) The middle 95% of the class ☐

(c) The bottom 2.5% of the class ☐

(q)

The level of marks was lower and the spread less this time around. My mark of 57 is above average and one more mark would have put me in the top 2.5%!

Got it?

Q: In a normal distribution, what percentage of observations are found within two standard deviations above and below the average for all observations?

A: 95%

Got it!

CONGRATULATIONS!

I am ....% confident
I understand the
95% rule!

Standard errors tell us how close to the real value a sample estimate is likely to be

Section 1

What is a standard error?

A

10 SEC summary

A standard error tells us how good any estimate of a population parameter provided by a random sample is likely to be.

60
SEC

summary

Sampling distributions produce standard errors

For some of the characteristics of a population, we can work out what estimate every random sample of a given size that could possibly be drawn from it would produce.

The distribution of these estimates is called a *sampling distribution* and it is approximately normal. The standard deviation of this distribution is called the *standard error*.

We can use this standard error to show how close a sample estimate is likely to be to the population parameter. A formula gives us the standard error for a proportion of any characteristic in the population.

We do not need to know anything about the real population parameters to do these calculations. This is the brilliance of inference.

In Petistan half the pets are dogs and half are cats.

We can calculate what happens when we draw every possible random sample of 1000 pets and find the proportion of cats in each one. (Don't worry about the maths of *how* we do this.)

This is called a *sampling distribution*. It is a distribution of sample estimates, instead of soldiers. Like the distribution of soldiers' heights discussed in the previous section, a sampling distribution is approximately normal.

DEFINING A SAMPLE DISTRIBUTION

This proportion of cats in each sample would range from 0 (all dogs) to 1 (all cats). Either result would be wildly unlikely, like tossing a far coin 1000 times and getting all heads, or picking a dwarf or giant soldier.

In the same way as soldiers would usually be of average height, most of the sample estimates would be very close to the proportion of cats in the target population, as shown in Figure 2.

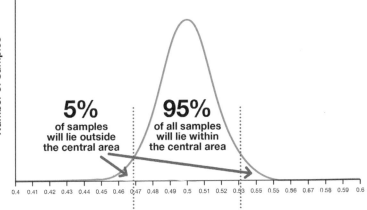

Figure 2 **Proportion of cats in the sample**

A formula defines the standard deviation of any sampling distribution for a proportion

$$\sqrt{(p(1-p)/n)}$$

where p is the proportion we are trying to measure and n is the size of the random sample we draw to measure it; $\sqrt{}$ means 'take the square root of'.

Thus in our example the standard deviation is

$$\sqrt{(0.5 \times 0.5/1000)} = \sqrt{0.00025} = 0.0158$$

CALCULATING STANDARD DEVIATIONS FOR SAMPLING DISTRIBUTIONS

In the same way as we did for the soldiers' heights, we use the mean and standard deviation of this sampling distribution to calculate the range of results for the proportion of cats that would be produced by the 95% of samples closest to the true value.

$0.5 + (2 \times 0.0158) = 0.53$

and

$0.5 - (2 \times 0.0158) = 0.47$

Hardly any samples would have a proportion of cats below 0.45 or above 0.55, and a staggeringly tiny number would have proportions below 0.4 or above 0.6. Samples like these would be like randomly picking a dwarf or giant soldier.

The standard deviation of a sampling distribution has a special name: the *standard error*.

GETTING YOUR HEAD AROUND STANDARD ERRORS AND SAMPLING DISTRIBUTIONS

Notice three things about the formula for the standard error of a sampling distribution

 It is not related at all to the size of the population.

2 It depends on the *square root* of the sample size. This means that increasing sampling accuracy requires an exponential increase in sample size.

3 Error does not mean *mistake*. It just describes how samples tend to vary.

THE STANDARD ERROR FORMULA

Look at what we just did

1 We did *not* need to know anything about the population. We just worked out what would happen *if* the pet population were evenly split between cats and dogs.

2 It was all in our *heads*. No cats or dogs were harmed in the production of our sampling distribution. We did not take any actual samples.

3 The standard error told us how close to a population parameter that a sample estimate was likely to be.

USING THE STANDARD ERROR FORMULA

PRACTISE THE STANDARD ERROR FORMULA

Get a calculator and try your hand with this new formula. I've done the first example.

Fill in the others.

Example

What is the range for 95% of samples if $p = 0.1$ and the sample size is 1000?

$$\sqrt{(p(1-p)/n)}$$

$$SE = \sqrt{0.1 \times (1-0.1) / 1000} = \sqrt{0.09 / 1000} = \sqrt{0.00009} = 0.0095$$

lower bound $= 0.1 - (2 \times 0.0095) = 0.081$

upper bound $= 0.1 + (2 \times 0.0095) = 0.119$

What is the range for 95% of sample estimates if $p = 0.5$ and sample size $n = 50$?

Using $\sqrt{(p(1-p)/n)}$

the standard error (SE) is

$$SE = \sqrt{(0.5 \times (1-0.5) / 50)} = \sqrt{(0.5 \times 0.5/ 50)}$$

$$= \sqrt{(0.25/50)} = \sqrt{0.005} = 0.071$$

Lower bound $= 0.5 - (2 \times 0.071) = 0.36$

Upper bound $= 0.5 + (2 \times 0.071) = 0.64$

A smaller sample makes the standard error larger and the 95% range of estimates wider.

CHECKPOINT

Over to you!

What is the range for 95% of samples if $p = 0.5$ and sample size $n = 10,000$?

$$SE = \sqrt{(0.5 \times 0.5/10,000)} = \sqrt{(0.25/10,000)} = \sqrt{0.000025} = 0.005$$

upper bound = $0.5 + (2 \times 0.005) = 0.51$

lower bound = $0.5 - (2 \times 0.005) = 0.49$

A larger sample makes the standard error smaller and the 95% range of estimates narrower.

What is the range for 95% of samples if $p = 0.1$ and sample size $n = 10,000$?

$$SE = \sqrt{(0.1 \times 0.9/10,000)} = \sqrt{(0.09/10,000)} = \sqrt{0.000009} = 0.003$$

upper bound = $0.1 + (2 \times 0.003) = 0.106$

lower bound = $0.1 - (2 \times 0.003) = 0.094$

Standard errors get smaller as the proportion we try to estimate gets closer to zero or one.

Section

5

Standard errors help us identify a range of estimates that we can be confident includes the population parameter

How do I
calculate
confidence
intervals with
standard
errors?

A

10 SEC summary

In 19 times out of 20 (95%) a *confidence interval* of two standard errors above and below a sample result will capture the true population parameter.

summary

Aim for 95% confidence

We only ever draw *one* random sample from a population, but knowing what the standard error of the sampling distribution is, we can work out where the population parameter is likely to lie.

We call our sample result a *point estimate*. It is our best guess of the true value of the population parameter.

We then draw a *confidence interval* two standard errors above and below our point estimate.

We can be 95% confident that this confidence interval contains the population parameter.

This confidence is about our procedure. Unfortunately it does not refer directly to our individual result.

GET YOUR HEAD AROUND POINT ESTIMATES

A sampling distribution only exists in our heads. Let's now actually draw a random sample of 1000 pets. We only draw *one* sample.

The proportion of cats in this sample becomes our point estimate for the proportion of cats in the population.

Just like picking one soldier, where the *single most probable* result would be to pick a soldier of average height, the single most probable sample, at the peak of the sampling distribution and the average for all samples, is one with the same proportion of cats as in the population.

Just like randomly picking a soldier, we'd still be very lucky to get such a result. Instead, as before, we can work out what would happen 95% of the time, using standard errors.

DETERMINING POINT ESTIMATES

If a range of two standard deviations either side of the mean of the sampling distribution contains 95% of samples, then it follows that if we take two standard deviations around the point estimate for our single sample, then 95% of the time our range will contain the unknown population parameter. This range is called a *confidence interval*.

When we count the cats in our sample, we find 450, a proportion of 0.45.

This is our best point estimate for the population parameter of the proportion of cats.

Using the same formula as before, for two standard errors

$$\sqrt{(0.45 \times 0.55/1000)} = \sqrt{(0.2475/1000)} = \sqrt{0.0002475}$$
$$= 0.0157 \times 2 = 0.031$$

Our confidence interval for the proportion of cats is therefore

0.419 to 0.481.

Figure 3 shows *four* different ways our sample might have come about.

VISUALIZING
YOUR SAMPLE

The red line shows the sampling distribution that would occur *if* the true proportion of cats in the population were 0.419 (0.45 minus two standard errors). The green line shows the sampling distribution if the true proportion were 0.481 (0.45 plus two standard errors).

Figure 3

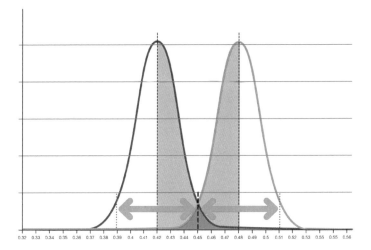

HOW CONFIDENCE INTERVALS RELATE TO SAMPLING

Our sample could be

- the sample with the *highest* proportion of cats in it from the 95% of samples nearest the true proportion when it is 0.419

- the sample with the *lowest* proportion of cats in it from the 95% of samples nearest the true proportion when it is 0.481

- a sample from the 95% of samples nearest the true proportion for *any value between* 0.419 and 0.481

- a sample from one of the 5% of samples from *any other* true proportion below 0.42 or above 0.48 that was more than two standard errors from the population proportion

We can therefore say we are *95% confident* that the proportion of cats in the population is between 0.419 and 0.481.

Note that there is nothing probable about the proportion of cats either in the population or in our sample. Probable cats do not exist!

PROBABLE PROCEDURES, NOT OBSERVATIONS

The proportion of cats in our sample is 0.45 with probability 100%. The proportion of cats in the pet population is either between 0.42 and 0.48, or it is not.

Similarly, when we randomly picked a soldier there was nothing probable about his height. Nor was there anything probable about the true average height of all soldiers.

What *is* probable is the *procedure* we have used to sample and measure the population. It is one that gives us a 95% chance of being within two standard errors of the true but unknown parameter value.

95% CONFIDENCE
IS NOT 100%

For any estimate we make, we cannot know if it is one of the 95% where the confidence interval captures the population parameter, or one of the 5% that misses.

Since 95% of observations actually lie 1.96 standard deviations either side of the mean in a normal distribution, rounding this figure to 2 makes our calculations easier.

UNDERSTANDING CONFIDENCE INTERVALS

You draw a sample of 10,000 pets.

You find it contains 4800 cats.

What is the 95% confidence interval (CI) for the proportion of cats in the pet population?

....

....

....

....

What does this confidence interval tell you?

....

....

....

....

$SE = \sqrt{p(1-p / n}$

$SE = \sqrt{0.48 \times 0.52 / 10000} = 0.005$

$1.96 \times 0.005 = 0.0098$

Upper limit of 95% CI = 0.480 + 0.0098 = 0.4898 = 0.490
Lower limit of 95% CI = 0.480 − 0.0098 = 0.4702 = 0.470

The interval tells us that, using the procedure we've followed (drawing a random sample of 10,000 pets), we can be 95% confident that the true proportion of cats in the pet population is between 0.47 and 0.49, or 47% and 49%.

Section

6

Testing a null
hypothesis

What is a
p-value?

A

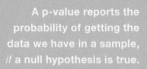

summary

A p-value reports the
probability of getting the
data we have in a sample,
if a null hypothesis is true.

summary

p-values, null hypotheses and probability

A *null hypothesis* (H_0) is any feature of the population for which we can produce a sampling distribution. Often the null hypothesis describes . what we would expect in our sample if there were no effect, no result or no relationship. We test a null hypothesis for the population by calculating the probability of getting the result we observe in our sample, *if* the hypothesis were true in the population.

This probability is called a *p-value*.

If this probability is *low* enough (equivalent to having a sample that must be at the extremes of the sampling distribution) we *reject* the null hypothesis. We may also *provisionally* accept that we have some kind of result, which we can describe as *statistically significant* and worthy of further investigation.

DETERMINING A NULL HYPOTHESIS

The Petistani Justice for Moggies! campaigns for a better life for cats, because they make up at least half the pet population. What does our sample estimate that the proportion of cats is only 0.45 mean for the campaigners?

Let's test a null hypothesis (H_0) about the population

$$H_0: \textit{at least half of all pets are cats}$$

WHAT GOOD IS A NULL HYPOTHESIS?

We can calculate the probability of getting the data we found in our sample, if this null hypothesis were true in the population. This is the same as asking, what proportion of all the possible random samples of size 1000 that we could draw from a population with 50% cats would contain a proportion of 0.45 cats or less?

The probability is about 0.001, since 0.5 is over three standard errors away from our point estimate of 0.45. It is well above 0.48, which was the upper limit of our confidence interval.

P-VALUES SIGNIFY PROBABILITY

This probability is a p-value: the probability of getting the data we would observe if our null hypothesis were true. If our data is *improbable* enough, given our hypothesis, we *reject* our null hypothesis.

What is 'improbable enough'? Conventionally a limit of 5% or 0.05 is used.

This is exactly the same as using a 95% confidence interval for point estimates.

Clearly 0.001 is less than 0.05, so we can *reject* our null hypothesis and declare a *statistically significant* result. We have *provisional* evidence that, contrary to the claims of Justice for Moggies!, there are in fact *fewer* cats than dogs in the population.

P-VALUES ONLY PROVIDE PROVISIONAL EVIDENCE

'Provisional' means we would be prepared to change our mind if new evidence appeared. Maybe after the sample was taken an epidemic decimated the dog population. Maybe another sample produces a very different result.

Just as with confidence intervals, significance refers to our procedure. Using this procedure, we would make the right decision on our hypothesis over 95 times out of 100.

But just like the soldiers, we cannot know if this particular decision was correct. Probable mistakes are as rare as probable cats or probable soldiers! Thus we talk about our level of confidence (95%) or we describe the level of significance (5%).

SET YOUR CONFIDENCE LEVEL BEFORE THE ANALYSIS

We adopt this roundabout procedure for two reasons

We can disprove what is false more easily than show what is true! We can calculate precisely the probability of getting our data if 50% of pets are cats. That is why we defined H_0 like that. Conversely, we do not know just how large the majority of dogs might be. Therefore we could not have produced a sampling distribution for it.

Our p-value reports the probability of our results, conditional upon H_0 being true: that is, $P(\text{Data} \mid H_0)$. We really want to know the probability of a hypothesis being true, conditional upon our data: that is, $P(H \mid \text{data})$. Unfortunately there is no way to calculate this.

USING P-VALUES TO TEST NULL HYPOTHESES

A researcher examines a sample of students to test the null hypothesis that women are more likely than men to live in single-sex flats. The researcher finds that the probability of the results, given a true null hypothesis, is 0.003. What should the researcher conclude based on the p-value?

....

....

....

....

The p-value is well below 0.05. Reject the null, provisionally – it looks as if men may be more likely to do so.

You organize a blind tasting of Coca-Cola and Pepsi, to see if your friend can tell the difference between them. On analysing the results you conclude that there was a 17% chance of your friend making as many correct calls as she did if she had just been guessing randomly. Your null hypothesis is that your friend cannot tell the difference. Do you reject it based on the p-value?

....

....

....

....

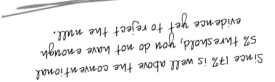

Since 17% is well above the conventional 5% threshold, you do not have enough evidence yet to reject the null.

p-values, confidence
and significance
describe how good our
procedures have been

What does a significant p-value actually mean?

A

10 SEC

summary

It tells us we have strong evidence against our null hypothesis – no more, no less.

A statistically significant result is only the beginning

Getting a low p-value and a statistically significant result are not the end of any research, but the beginning. They are useful indicators of which leads to follow up.

However, it is vital to remember that, by definition, 5% of statistically significant findings will be wrong. We just don't know which ones. The p-values, confidence and significance only describe how good our procedures for getting that information have been.

THE FOUR POSSIBLE RESULTS OF HYPOTHESIS TESTING

We reject a null hypothesis that is in fact false... **Correct!**

If there are more dogs in the Petistani population this is what we have done.

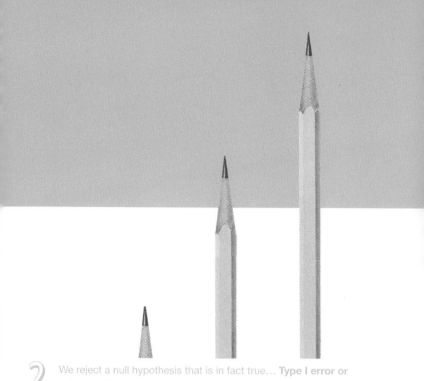

2 We reject a null hypothesis that is in fact true... **Type I error or false positive.**

Perhaps there are in fact as many cats as dogs, but our sample was one of the 0.1% of random samples that could be drawn from this population with a proportion of 0.45 cats or less. We have rejected a null hypothesis that is actually true.

We accept a null hypothesis that is in fact true... **Correct!**

Say we had found that the proportion of cats in our sample was 0.49. We would not have had enough evidence to reject the possibility that there were as many cats as dogs. If there were equal numbers of cats and dogs in the population we would have made the right call.

4. We accept a null hypothesis that is in fact false... **Type II error or false negative.**

However, if there were fewer cats in the population, and either we had been unlucky with our sample, or the difference in cat and dog numbers was so small that our sample was not big enough to find it, accepting the null would have been the wrong call.

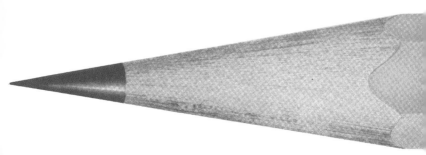

EFFECT AND SAMPLE SIZE MATTER

The stronger the *effect* or relationship we are looking for, the easier it is for random sample data to pick it up. Imagine the real proportion of cats in the pet population was only 25%. How big a random sample would we need to have a high probability of rejecting a null hypothesis of an equal number of cats and dogs?

Even with a sample of only 100 pets our chances of getting 50% or more of cats in our sample would be infinitesimal. With a sample of just 20 pets we would still have enough evidence to reject the null with 95% confidence, simply because the preponderance of dogs was so great.

Type I and II errors are a trade-off

We can reduce our risk of making Type I errors or false positive results by demanding lower p-values. However, this will result in a higher risk of Type II errors and missing some true positive results! Any level of significance that we decide upon is a compromise between these two risks.

A P-VALUE DOES NOT MEASURE HYPOTHESIS PROBABILITY

Finally we must keep in mind just what a p-value means. It tells us the probability of getting our sample data, *if* the null hypothesis we are testing is true in the population.

It does not tell us the probability that our null hypothesis is true. Just like the height of an individual soldier, there is nothing probable about any hypothesis. Either it is true or it is not.

What is probable is our knowledge about it. Confidence intervals, significance levels and p-values tell us how good our sample evidence is in making inferences about a population. Because we cannot measure that population, we describe our knowledge of it in terms of probability. These probabilities tell us how good our procedures have been and how strong our evidence is likely to be as a result. However, they cannot ever totally guarantee that any individual result is in fact correct.

Look at each of the following statements and decide if they are true or false

1 A p-value describes the Type I error rate   True / False

2 A p-value describes the probability of making the wrong decision if you reject the null hypothesis   True / False

3 A p-value describes the probability that the null hypothesis is true   True / False

4 A statistically significant result proves that the null hypothesis is false   True / False

5 Rejecting a null hypothesis means claiming a statistically significant result   True / False

6 A p-value is the probability of getting the result observed if the null hypothesis is true in the population from which the random sample was drawn   True / False

7 A result which is not significant proves that the null hypothesis is true   True / False

8 A significant result is an important result   True / False

ANSWERS

1 TRUE

2 FALSE

3 FALSE

4 FALSE

5 TRUE

6 TRUE

7 FALSE

8 FALSE

CONGRATULATIONS!
I AM A P-VALUE PRO!

#LittleQuickFix

☐ Can you describe the difference between statistical significance and importance? If not, look back at page 12–15.

☐ Do you know the difference between a population parameter and a sample estimate? If not, look back at page 13.

☐ Can you define a random sample and why you need one? If not, look back at page 27.

☐ Do you know which two numbers define a normal distribution? If not, look back at page 37.

HOW TO KNOW
YOU
ARE
DONE

Do you know what a standard error is? If not, look back at page 61.

Do you know how to calculate and use a confidence interval? If not, look back at page 75.

Do you know what probability a p-value describes? If not, look back at page 91.

Do you know what a p-value actually means and what Type I and Type II errors are? If not, look back at page 105.

Get all these right (even if it means going back to check) and there is a high probability that we can reject the null hypothesis that you know nothing about statistical significance (p < 0.01)!

Glossary

Confidence The probability in the long run of a sampling procedure producing a correct result.

Confidence interval Give a level of confidence, the range of values within which a population parameter is estimated to lie.

False negative Deciding a result is not statistically significant when it would indeed have been found in the target population.

False positive Deciding a result is statistically significant when it would not be found in the target population.

Histogram A graphic that displays a continuous variable, in which the area corresponding to a range of values equals the proportion of all observations in that value range.

Hypothesis A statement about a population.

Inference The process of making statements about or descriptions of a population based on analysis of a random sample drawn from it.

Mean The arithmetic average of a group of values.

n The number of observations, e.g. in a sample.

Normal distribution A symmetrical distribution in which the mode, median and mean values coincide, and the proportion of observations decline as their distance from the mean increases.

Null hypothesis A statement about a population for which a sampling distribution can be constructed.

p-value The probability of obtaining a result or measurement if the null hypothesis is true for the population.

Parameter A characteristic of a population, e.g. proportion, mean, standard deviation, etc.

Point estimate An estimate of the value of a population parameter taken from a random sample.

Random sample A sample in which every member of a population has a known probability of being selected.

Sampling distribution The distribution of the estimate for a population parameter produced by all random samples of size *n* drawn from a population.

Sigma (σ) Greek letter and symbol for the standard deviation.

Square root A number which multiplied by itself produces the original number, e.g. $\sqrt{9} = 3$, $\sqrt{4} = 2$

Standard deviation A measure of the dispersion of a range of values, in which a higher value indicates more dispersion.

Standard error The standard deviation of a sampling distribution.

Statistical significance Results in a sample are described as 'significant' if the probability of obtaining them, were a null hypothesis actually true in the population, is small enough.

(Target) population A collection of people, objects, measurements or anything else that is of interest to us.

Type I and II errors Type I: false positive = reject true null hypothesis. Type II: false negative = accept false null hypothesis.